Let's Go Shopping

Written by Betty Moon
Illustrated by Jamie Oliver
Photographed by Steve Lumb

Collins

We go to the shoe shop ...

... to get trainers.

shoe shop

We go to the bakery ...

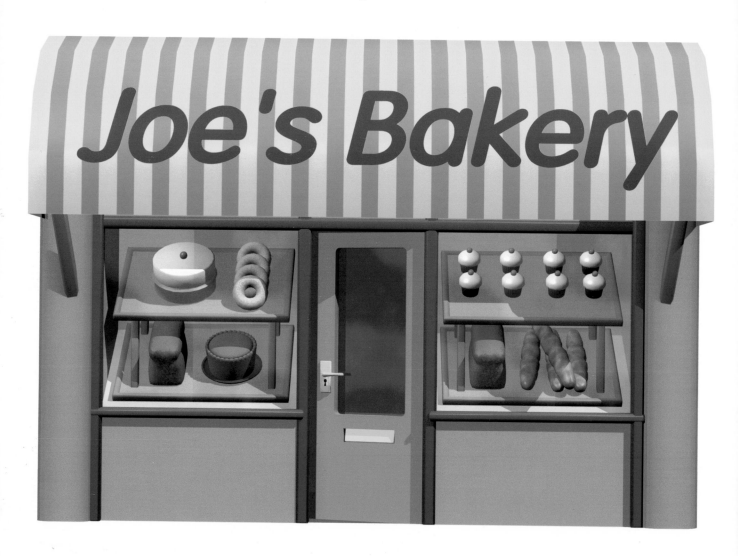

... to get bread.

bakery

We go to the bookshop ...

... to get books.

book shop

We go to the newsagent ...

... to get a comic.

newsagent

We go to the café ...

... to get a drink.

café

We go to the supermarket ...

... to get all sorts of things!

supermarket

A shopping map

bookshop

bakery

shoe shop

Joe's Bakery

supermarket

14

15

✸ Ideas for guided reading ✸

Learning objectives: Recognising printed and handwritten words in a variety of settings, e.g. labels, signs, notices; reading on sight high frequency words; advertisements, newspapers; expecting written text to make sense and to check for sense if it does not; know more phoneme-grapheme correspondences: *sh*; describe incidents or tell stories from their own experience.

Curriculum links: Knowledge and Understanding of the World: Observe, find out about and identify features in the place they live and the natural world

Interest words: shoe, shop, trainers, bakery, bread, book shop, books, supermarket, sorts, things, newsagent, comic, café, drink

High frequency words: We, go, get, all, to, the, of, a

Word count: 55

Getting started

- Read the title together and ask the children about their experiences of shopping, e.g. *What happens when you go shopping?* Ask each to tell the whole group, speaking clearly and concisely.

- Ask the children where they would go to get certain products, e.g. books, shoes, bread. Point out that we go to certain shops for certain things.

- Walk through the book and discuss what is happening – it is about two children shopping at different shops. Prompt children to watch as the shopping bag fills up. *Have you been to these shops before?*

Reading and responding

- Ask the children to read independently and aloud. Observe and prompt their use of initial letters and the pictures. Prompt them to read other words on the page such as signs and labels.

- Before turning each page, encourage children to say what else they could have bought at that shop, e.g. a newspaper at the newsagent's.